No Limits

SKATEBOARDING

Jed Morgan

A⁺

Smart Apple Media

First published in 2005 by Franklin Watts
96 Leonard Street, London EC2A 4XD

Franklin Watts Australia
45–51 Huntley Street, Alexandria NSW 2015

This edition published under license from Franklin Watts. All rights reserved.
Copyright © 2005 Franklin Watts

Series editor: Adrian Cole, Series design: Pewter Design Associates, Art director: Jonathan Hair,
Picture researcher: Sophie Hartley

Acknowledgements:
The publisher acknowledges all © products shown within this title as the property of their respective owners. Tony Donaldson/Action Plus: 29t. Tim Leighton-Boyce/Action Plus: Cover. ©Bettmann/Corbis: 4. © Strauss/ Curtis/Corbis: 14t. © John-Marshall Mantel/Corbis: 13tr. © Mike McGill/Corbis: 14b, 21b. © Al Fuchs/ NewSport/Corbis: 17r, 21tr, 26b, 28t. © Matthew Kasperek/NewSport/Corbis: 8t. © Rick Rickman/NewSport/ Corbis: 10. © Eric Perlman/Corbis: 9b. © Phil Schermeister/Corbis: 5tl. © Ted Soqui/Corbis: 23b. © Paul A. Souders/Corbis: 15. © Michael S. Yamashita/Corbis: 26t. © Jess Dyrenforth: 8b, 18, 19t, 24, 27b. Kim Myung Jung Kim/PA/Empics: 28b. Last Resort Picture Library: 12, 13cl, 20, 22t & b, 23t. Courtesy Lush Longboards Ltd.: 9t. ©Styley/PYMCA: 25t. David Thorpe/Rex Features: 5tr. Courtesy Shiner Ltd. www.shiner.co.uk: 5b, 6–7 all, 11 all, 13tl, bl & br, 25b. © Patty Segovia/Silver Photo Agency: 16, 21tl, 29b. Courtesy DannyWay.com, Photo by Blabac. © DC Shoes Inc.: 17l, 27t. Courtesy DannyWay.com, © 2004 Tony Vu/Shazaam/ESPN Images: 19b.

Published in the United States by Smart Apple Media
2140 Howard Drive West, North Mankato, Minnesota 56003

U.S. publication copyright © 2007 Smart Apple Media
International copyright reserved in all countries. No part of this book may be reproduced in any form without written permission from the publisher.
Printed in the United States of America

Library of Congress Cataloging-In-Publication Data

Morgan, Jed.
Skateboarding / by Jed Morgan.
p. cm. — (No limits)
Originally published: London : Franklin Watts, 2005.
Includes index.
ISBN-13 : 978-1-58340-959-6
1. Skateboarding—Juvenile literature. I. Title.

GV859.8.M67 2006
796.22—dc22   2005052555

9 8 7 6 5 4 3 2 1

Important Note:

Disclaimer—In the preparation of this book, all due care has been exercised with regard to the activities depicted. The publishers regret that they can accept no liability for any loss or injury sustained.

Contents

World of skateboarding 4

Know your skateboard 6

A skateboard for all 8

Get geared up 10

Get ready to go 12

Play it safe 14

Just for fun 16

Skateboarding sports 18

Getting started 20

Moving on 22

Advanced tricks 24

Get serious! 26

Meet the pros 28

Jargon buster 30

Find out more 31

Index 32

World of skateboarding

Whether you want to jam in the local skatepark or just goof around with friends, skateboarding is a great way to get around in today's busy world.

Skateboarding is born

As far back as the early 1900s, people were experimenting with early skateboards by attaching roller skate wheels to pieces of wood. The big break for skateboards came in the early 1960s, when Larry Stevenson began to promote the skateboard for "surfing the streets" in the United States. In 1963, his company, Mahaka, made the first professional skateboards. Within just a few years, more than 50 million skateboards had been sold.

To the limit

Early skateboards had clay wheels that offered little grip. Several accidents (including some deaths) and a public outcry about dangerous skateboarders led to a decline in the sport after 1965.

Four boys surf the streets on their skateboards in Chicago, Illinois, in 1965.

Plastic Fantastic

Frank Nasworthy introduced new plastic (polyurethane) wheels in 1973, which gave skateboards much greater control. The new wheels led to a skateboard boom, and by 1976, the sport had its own magazines and its first skateboard park in Florida. By 1980, the craze for new BMX bikes saw skateboarding decline in popularity again. But hardcore boarders kept the sport alive, and today it is more popular than ever.

Skateboarding a concrete bowl in the 1970s. The development of polyurethane wheels led to a new surge in skateboarding.

Ready on the ramp in the 1980s. Skateboard fashion has changed over the years.

FROM THE EDGE

"Skateboarding has not yet reached its maximum potential, and who can say what the limits are? To find out, grab that board! You don't have to be a super-talented professional skater—grab that board if you're a novice just having some fun on a Saturday afternoon." Extract from the first edition of *Thrasher* skateboard magazine, 1981

Thrasher *magazine today. Many skateboard magazines have helped to promote the sport.*

The skateboard craze

Besides magazines, there are now skateboarding films, Web sites, and even computer games, as well as thousands of skateboard shops. The sport now has worldwide competitions, including its own showcase, the X-Games. It is a billion-dollar industry, with top pros earning thousands of dollars in prize and sponsorship money.

Know your skateboard

Today, skateboards use the latest materials and technology to provide the ultimate ride. This Bullet Bird shares four basic elements with all skateboards—the deck, trucks, wheels, and bearings.

GRIP TAPE
The top of the deck has a gritty covering called grip tape, which helps your feet grip the board.

DECK
✱ Usually made of seven layers (plies) of maple wood that are glued together (laminated) and shaped under high-pressure.

✱ Decks can be up to nine-ply, which makes them stronger, but also heavier.

✱ Deck width — A good all-around deck is eight inches (20.3 cm) wide. Wider decks of up to eight and a half inches (21.6 cm) are preferred by vert or ramp skaters, while street and trick skaters use narrower decks of seven and a half to seven and three-quarters inches (19–19.7 cm).

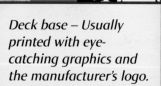

Deck base – Usually printed with eye-catching graphics and the manufacturer's logo.

SHOCK PADS

These rubber pads fit between the base of the deck and the top of the trucks. They help reduce shocks for a smoother ride.

King pin

Axle

Base plate

Bushing

TRUCKS

✴ Trucks bolt to the base of your deck and hold the wheels.

✴ They are made up of several parts but are usually sold as a unit.

✴ The axle length of trucks varies, but the axle should not stick out beyond the rail of your deck (unless you have a longboard).

✴ Long axles make the board turn more slowly.

✴ Short axles make the board turn quickly.

✴ Trucks have an adjustable plastic bushing that works a bit like a shock absorber and controls the feel of the board. The tighter you make the bushing, the harder your turns will feel.

Truck – five inches (125 mm), nonslip axle, high-grade aluminum

Wheel – 54–mm (2 in.) bulletproof polyurethane
Bearings – ABEC3

HOT HINT

Complete or custom-built? It is easy to build your own skateboard by buying all of the parts separately. This is well worth it as you get into skateboarding. A custom board can be expensive, though, so if you're just starting out, buy a complete board. This will be good enough to learn on and will give you time to plan and save up for your perfect board!

Cool science

Bearings fit inside the wheel and allow it to spin freely around the axle. There are many types, and most—but not all—are rated with a number (usually 1, 3, 5, or 7). The higher the number, the faster the bearing will turn. Bearings are a standard size and will fit any wheel.

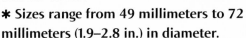

WHEELS

Wheels are made from polyurethane compound (a type of plastic) and vary in size and hardness.

✴ Sizes range from 49 millimeters to 72 millimeters (1.9–2.8 in.) in diameter.

✴ Large wheels help increase speed and stability.

✴ Small wheels are better for tricks and street skating.

✴ Hardness is measured in durometers from 99 (the softest) to 101 (the hardest). Hard wheels are faster and last longer, but soft wheels give a smoother ride.

A skateboard for all

Choosing the right skateboard depends on what you want to do with it. Skateboard shop staff members will help you consider all of the options, but here is the lowdown on the main board types.

HOT HINT

Remember that most skateboarding components will fit any deck. Try swapping parts with friends and see what board setup best suits you.

Vert boards

If you want to spend most of your time perfecting those vert ramps, these are the boards for you. A vert board is wider than a standard board, with a deck of eight and a quarter to eight and a half inches (21–21.6 cm). Larger and softer wheels are usually chosen by vert riders, as they give greater stability for riding the ramps.

Vert boards, such as this one, are wider to give greater stability on ramps.

Street boards give the rider greater control during tricks, such as this kickflip.

Street/Technical boards

If you're going to be skating around town, then you'll need one of these boards. Street, or technical, skating involves lots of grinds, flip tricks, and other technical moves. Street boards have a narrower deck of around seven and a half to eight inches (19–20.3 cm) and smaller, harder wheels to make it easier to flip the board or perform jumps.

Cruisers

If you will mainly use your skateboard for cruising, then it's best to get a longer deck. This will give you greater balance and control. Larger and softer wheels will increase your speed and help you ride out bumps and cracks in the pavement. For serious cruising, you may want to choose a longboard.

Longboards

These are longer skateboards that range in length from around 36 inches (91.4 cm) to a whopping 60 inches (152.4 cm)! The decks are often shaped with a more pointed nose and tail than other decks and are also wider in the middle—nine inches (23 cm) or more. The trucks and wheels on many longboards stick out beyond the edge of the deck. This gives greater maneuverability and keeps the wheels from catching the board when carving (turning) at high speeds. Longboards are the speed freak's dream and are great for cruising.

Lush longboard "Legend."

FROM THE EDGE

"Longboards, with their smooth-turning trucks and fast wheels, give a flowing, carving ride that can be everything from chilled-out cruising to extreme, high-speed slides, depending on your mood. The Legend has a 48-inch (122 cm) deck and features Lush L125 trucks, Kryptonics 65-millimeter (2.6 in.) wheels, and Lush Swiss ABEC5 bearings."
Lush Web site (www.lushlongboards.com)

Mountain boards aren't really skateboards at all, but they use skateboard technology.

Mountain boards

Mountain boards use skateboard technology but have adapted it for off-road boarding by adding specialized trucks and air-filled tires. The boards are long and use materials such as fiberglass, carbon fiber, and wood. This is to keep them strong but lightweight. Mountain boards also have a binding system similar to that on a snowboard. This straps your feet to the board and improves your board control.

Get geared up

There is more skateboard gear than there are skateboards, but it is not just about looking good. Skateboard gear is designed to let you skate to your limits and stay in one piece at the same time.

Skate shoes

You can skate in any shoe, but skate shoes will dramatically improve your comfort and performance. They are made of soft materials to let your foot flex and have wide, flat soles with sticky rubber to help you stay on the deck. Skate shoes have become popular as a general street fashion in recent years, so there are now hundreds to choose from. Your local skate store will help you select the right ones for you.

Many skateboarders wear skate-style shoes. The wide soles greatly enhance rider performance.

Patches

These are a great way to customize your clothing to fit your own image. They are produced by a wide range of manufacturers and are available from all good skateboard shops.

Clothes

There are no rules with skateboard clothing. Some skaters prefer shorts, others pants. Some like hooded tops, known as "hoodies," while others choose T-shirts. The most important thing is that you feel comfortable. For most skaters, a pair of loose-fitting jeans (to allow movement) and a cotton T-shirt are ideal.

HOT HINT

If you can't find a T-shirt or hoodie you like, why not design your own and have it printed? This doesn't cost much and makes you stand out from the crowd. Many skateboard pros have developed their own designs.

Helmet

Concussions and other head injuries can be avoided if you wear a helmet. There are so many helmets to choose from that there's no excuse for not having one. They are lightweight and fully ventilated, so they won't affect your skateboarding performance. Ask the staff at your local skate shop to make sure your helmet is a good fit. Wearing an incorrectly fitted helmet is almost as bad as not wearing one at all. If you take any serious hits, get your helmet checked out and replace it if necessary.

Pads and guards

Even if you think a grazed elbow looks cool, knee and elbow pads provide vital protection. These are the parts most likely to scrape along the ground when you fall. Knee pads are particularly important in vert skating, so that you can slide down the ramp on them when you fail to land a trick. Some pads can be worn under your clothing. Wrist guards are gloves with a rib of metal or toughened plastic inside. They should be worn whatever your skate style.

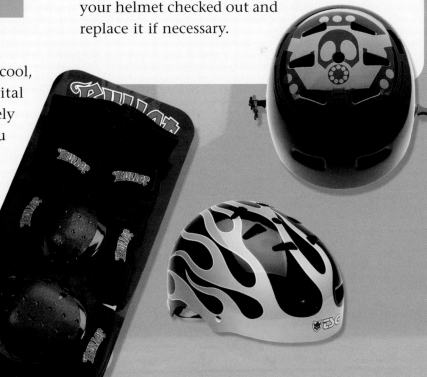

Get ready to go

The best riders work as one with their boards. They provide the energy, steering, and lift that are needed to make the board perform to its limit. Your body will do a lot of the work, so it's important to get it ready for action.

A good stretch

Stretches are a way of preparing your muscles for work. Move slowly into each stretch and hold it for about 15 seconds. Repeat each stretch several times on each side of your body. Hip and hamstring stretches are the most useful for skateboarding.

A hamstring stretch helps a rider warm up his muscles.

Hips

Stand with your feet slightly apart and your arms stretched out ahead. Keeping your lower body still, rotate slowly from the waist to one side and then the other. Next, put your hands on your hips and lean over to the side. Do this several times and repeat on the other side. Keeping your hands on your hips, gently rotate your hips in a circle.

Hamstring

Stand with your legs apart, and put both hands together. Bend at the waist, and try to touch the ground between your legs. Repeat several times, but come up each time—don't bounce! Now try to touch each toe by reaching to the side as you bend. Repeat several times on each side.

Board Fit

Always check out your board before you head out (see below right). It won't need much maintenance, but eventually parts will wear out, and they'll need to be replaced. Always keep spare parts handy so you can get skating right away. These parts include rubber bushings and metal retainer cups (1), truck bolts (2), and axle nuts (3).

A board sustains damage when you perform tricks. Remember to check yours before riding it.

Customize your board

Customizing your board is the easiest thing in the world and can be done cheaply by using manufacturers' stickers (right). Next time you replace your wheels, check out the full range. Wheels are a distinctive way to make your board stand out. You could even update your trucks to bring new life to your old board.

HOT HINT

Before you head out:

1. DECK — Never ride a board if you think it is damaged—ask the staff at your local skate shop to check it out if you're not sure. ✓

2. GRIP TAPE — Make sure the grip tape on the deck is clean. Brush off any excess dirt. ✓

3. WHEELS — Make sure they are not worn; replace them if big chunks of polyurethane are missing. Make sure the wheels spin freely—service or replace noisy bearings. ✓

4. TRUCKS — Check the mounting hardware (truck bolts, etc.) to make sure it's tight. ✓

5. AXLE NUTS — Make sure these are secure; suddenly skating on three wheels isn't fun. ✓

Play it safe

Skateboarding is all about having fun and pushing yourself to the extremes, but it can be dangerous to yourself and others. By following some simple guidelines and playing it safe, you can avoid most problems.

Look after yourself

All the padding in the world will not protect you if you try to out-trick yourself. Don't be in a rush to perfect your skating style. It is far better to take things slowly and master each level of skill as you go. If you can, try out new moves on a soft surface, such as grass, as this will help cushion your fall. Don't be afraid to ask for advice from more experienced skaters.

HOT HINT

"Don't skate foolishly—think about what you're doing all the time. Use your head; that's the best piece of safety advice I can give—stay alert, stay alive."
Bethany Green, skateboard instructor

Some street skaters don't wear safety gear. It's a choice they make, but if you don't wear it, the risks of injury are much higher.

Look out for others

You will often find yourself practicing tricks and skating in public places. In recent years, some skateboarders have given the sport a bad name by ignoring the safety of others. Thankfully, most skateboarders today behave responsibly. Remember to share spaces with other skaters and always give way to pedestrians. The elderly, very young, and animals can find a fast-approaching skateboard especially frightening.

Respect the rules

Skateboarding has been banned from some busy public areas, but there are special parks you can use. If you don't know where these parks are, ask your local council for information. Many skaters are pushing for special skate zones, but these will only be granted if skaters respect the rules that already exist. You should always be careful not to trespass onto private property even if it has irresistible steps, rails, and walls for jumps and grinds.

Skateboarding a new ramp in Oslo, Norway. Some authorities have built public skateboarding areas.

FROM THE EDGE

"Cities and municipalities have an obligation to their communities to provide safe places for their youth to skate. It is an investment in their future."
Skate Park Association of the United States of America (SPAUSA)

Skate smart

Safety tips for skateboarders:
* Make sure all equipment is in good condition and fits properly.
* Always wear a helmet, and replace it every two to three years or after a major impact.
* Wrist guards will help to prevent wrist fractures in case of falls.
* Choose a safe location away from traffic.
* Learn how to control your speed and stop.
* Do not wear headphones.
* Do not skate at night or in wet conditions.
* STAY ALERT! Keep your eyes on the surface ahead; watch for other people, cars, and hazards such as cracks and rocks.
* Respect others around you.

Just For Fun

Skateboarding may well be a billion-dollar international sport, but most skaters do it just for fun. For millions, skateboarding is simply a way to get together with board buddies.

HOT HINT

If you want to try skateboarding but can't rent or borrow a board, check the notice boards in local skate shops. You could pick up a second-hand board for next to nothing. Check that it's street-worthy before handing over your cash.

Rent or borrow

If you are tempted by skateboarding but don't want to splash out on your own board just yet, then try renting or borrowing one. Find out if your local skatepark has a rental program. Better yet, see if you can borrow one from a more experienced skater. There is a good chance he or she will have more than one. By renting or borrowing, you can check out the sport before spending your cash. Be warned, though: skateboarding is the only thing you'll want to do once you've tried it!

Free Fun

The best thing about skateboarding is that once you have a basic board and safety gear, it is a virtually free sport. You can wear whatever you want and skate wherever you are allowed to. The only costs will be your maintenance costs and those tempting upgrades.

The All Girl Skate Jam holds regular events for "all ages, all abilities, all girls."

Skate clubs

Take your skateboard experience to another level by joining a skateboard club in your area. Many of them arrange regular jams and may even have their own vert ramps. A club can also be a great place to pick up tricks and tips, and to meet new skaters. If there is no club in your area, why not get together with your buddies and start your own?

FROM THE EDGE

"Just go out there and have fun and do what you normally do. If you go out there and your main purpose is to get a sponsor, then it's not gonna work. Just go out there and have fun. That's how I got sponsored." Ryan Sheckler (right), pro skateboarder and X-Games gold medalist

Danny Way grabs some air. Skateboard events are held across the world and attract all the pros.

Skateboard events

There is nothing that beats the thrill of watching real skateboard pros in action. You will be amazed at how high they can jump and how fast they can travel. The best chance to see them is at a regional, national, or international competition, but these might be too far away for you to get to. Another good way to catch them is to keep an eye out for special events in your area. Skateboarding manufacturers often put together showcase events. They invite pros who show off the products in action. Your local skate shop or club will probably know of upcoming events, so go along and be inspired.

Skateboarding sports

Skateboarding can be divided into several different sports, each with its own specialized skills. All of them test speed, strength, timing, and nerves.

Vert skating gives riders the chance to pull tricks that aren't possible any other way.

Vert skating

If you like the look of seriously big air, then vert skating is the sport for you. Vert (meaning vertical) skaters use halfpipes to build up speed and pull tricks before trying to land back on the ramp. Most skateparks have at least one vert ramp and may have several of differing sizes. A normal ramp is around 11.5 feet (3.5 m) high and about 30 feet (9 m) wide, but ramps vary greatly and each has its own challenges. In recent years, top skaters have pushed beyond the vert ramp to the super ramp (20 feet, or 6 m, high) and now even the mega ramp, with a halfpipe more than 26 feet (8 m) high!

To the limit

Using the mega ramp that he invented, skater Danny Way holds the World Record for the longest skateboard jump of 78.7 feet (24 m) and the biggest air of more than 23 feet (7 m).

Street skating

This is the most popular form of skateboarding today because you can do it almost anywhere. The curbs, walls, steps, and rails that are found in any town or city are all challenging obstacles to the street skater. The streets outside the South Bank arts center in London have been a favorite hangout for street skaters since the 1970s. Many people have complained about skaters damaging the area, but in 2004, a series of five "skateable" sculptures was introduced, and skateboarding was officially welcomed on the South Bank. Not everywhere is as welcoming to street skaters, though. Make sure you check out where is hot and where not to skate.

This street layout has been created for a competition.

FROM THE EDGE

"I didn't plan on breaking any records; I'm just stoked to see skateboarding progress and go to a higher level. . . ." Danny Way (below) after breaking the longest air world record at the X-Games in August 2004

Slalom skateboarding

This is one of the oldest types of skateboarding and was popular in the 1960s and 1970s. Riders have to pass down a course through a number of gates (usually cones) in the fastest time possible. Most races are against the clock, with the fastest rider winning. Slalom skateboarding began a comeback in 2001, with the first World Championships in nearly 20 years. Its popularity has also been helped by the new longboards—perfect for fast turns. There are now regular races across the U.S. and Europe.

Getting started

Once you have your board, you will be desperate to pull those big air tricks, but it is important to master the basics first. They will make you a better rider and keep you from getting injured, too.

Get the stance

Stand sideways on the skateboard with your feet spaced about shoulder-width apart. Keep your knees slightly bent, and use your arms to help keep your balance. Always look where you are going and not down at your feet! You will hear riders talk about a regular or goofy foot. If you stand with your left foot in front, then you are a regular rider, but if your right foot is in front, then you're a goofy.

Feel the board

The first trick you must learn is to get used to the feel of moving on a board and wheels! The most important thing is to stay relaxed—this will help your body flex and improve your balance. Put your skateboard on a soft surface (lawn or carpet), and try standing on it to get used to its feel. Try different stances until you figure out what suits you best. If you need to, ask someone to steady you until you are more confident.

Finding your balance

Skateboarding is all about good balance. Find a flat surface, and start off with your front foot on the board. Push slowly with your back foot, and get used to the feel of the movement. When you are confident, push again, and when you are moving, lift your back foot onto the deck—now you are skateboarding! Next, try some simple crouching movements as you go along. Bend your knees to go slowly down and then up again. Use your arms to keep your balance. This crouching movement is a key move that you will use in many tricks, such as the Ollie (see page 23).

Balancing skills are key to every skateboard move. Practice on flat ground before attempting a ramp like this one.

Falling and bailing

You can't practice tricks without falling. The main thing to remember is to scrunch up and allow yourself to roll, or to use your pads to land. Your board can become a serious hazard, especially if you land on it. If you feel yourself falling during a trick, bail by kicking your board out of the way.

HOT HINT

Try not to put your hands out when you fall, especially on the vert ramp. It's an automatic reaction, but you are more likely to damage your wrists or hands, or even break an arm. Wear wrist guards to reduce the chance of getting injured.

Moving on

When you feel comfortable on your board, it's time to take it up a notch and move on to some key moves and essential tricks. Don't expect to learn these overnight, though—even the experts spent many hours learning the basics.

Turning

The trucks and wheels of your skateboard do most of the turning work for you. How quickly you turn will depend on your setup. Loose-set trucks and small wheels will give sharper turns but are not as stable. The main thing you have to learn is controlling your weight to start and end a turn. To begin a turn, simply shift your weight toward the side of the board you want to turn; your trucks will do the rest. To straighten out, shift your weight back again.

Tic tac

In this trick, you move the nose of your board from side to side by shifting your weight onto the tail of the board so that the nose lifts off the ground. With the nose in the air, you can easily pivot your board from side to side. Your front foot controls how high the nose lifts. To come down again, simply put your weight back over the nose. The tic tac is good for learning basic weight control.

The Ollie

This is the skateboard jump and the starting point for nearly all skateboard tricks. Popping an Ollie is all about timing and takes a while to master. It is best to learn by watching others, but here are the basics.

✳ Ride along with your back foot on the tail of the deck (your front foot will be somewhere in the middle) and your knees bent in a crouch position.

✳ Kick down on the tail to make the board hit the ground, and as the front pops up, jump with it. As you do so, slide your front foot up the grip tape toward the nose. This will help lift the board and level it out in midair. Gravity will bring you down again!

✳ Straighten your legs a little to meet the ground, and then bend them as you touch down to help absorb the impact.

To the limit

The Ollie is named after Alan "Ollie" Gelfand, who invented the most important move in skateboarding back in 1977 when he was just 14 years old.

To the limit

Danny Wainwright of Britain popped an Ollie of nearly four feet (1.13 m) in February 2000—the highest ever recorded.

FROM THE EDGE

"When he [Alan Gelfand] reached the top of the bowl, he used his back foot to horse-kick his tail. This act shot the tail of his board, almost crashing it into the concrete lip. It seemed the harder he kicked it, the higher his board would pop, or "Ollie." I was amazed. I'd never seen anything like that before, and he did it so fast and effortlessly." Stacy Peralta (left) describing Alan "Ollie" Gelfand inventing the Ollie in 1977.

Advanced tricks

Most tricks take time to master. They can also be quite risky, so you should not try them until you are ready. It is a good idea to take lessons from someone more experienced. The 50–50 Grind and kickflip are two popular tricks.

The 50–50 Grind

This is a key street skating move, in which you ride your skateboard along an edge, such as a curb or rail, using the trucks instead of the wheels. You will need to know how to do an Ollie before you try this trick.

✱ Choose what it is you want to grind, and skate alongside it.

✱ When you have picked up some speed (not too fast!), pop an Ollie and aim to land your trucks on the edge you want to grind.

✱ Bend your legs as you land to absorb the impact, and try not to land too heavily, or the board may just stop instead of grinding.

✱ As your board slows and you come to the end of your grind, pop another small Ollie to jump off the object and back to your wheels.

✱ Start with small obstacles, such as a low curb, and you will soon master the 50–50 Grind. Then you can move on to try other grinds such as the 5–0 Grind (a grind on the rear truck only) and the Nosegrind (using the front truck only).

50–50 Grind. Nothing beats the feeling of achieving a good grind.

HOT HINT

To extend the length of your grinds, first apply curb wax to the object. It's also a good idea to watch for traces of wax to see what other riders have been grinding.

To the limit

Curt Lindgren invented the first "old-school" kickflip in the 1970s, when it was used by freestyle riders as part of their flatland display (tricks performed without ramps). Variations of the old-school kickflip include the M–80, the 180 Kickflip, and the Helicopter.

The kickflip

This move was invented by skating legend Rodney Mullen in 1982 and is an adaption of Lindgren's old-school kickflip. Mullen's kickflip makes your board flip 360 degrees while you are above it in midair. To pull a kickflip:

✳ Pop a good Ollie—you will need some height for this, so perfect your Ollie first.

✳ As you drag your front foot up the grip tape, flick it off the heel side of your board to set the board into a sideways flip. Make sure you take your back foot off the deck so that it can flip.

✳ Stay above the board and, as it completes the flip, land with your back foot first to keep the board from over-flipping.

✳ Remember to flex your knees for a smooth landing, and use your arms to help you balance.

In midair during a kickflip. You'll need good air to nail this trick.

HOT HINT

There are instructional DVDs that can show you how to attempt most tricks. Many feature top skateboarding pros and go through the trick step-by-step. However, the only way to really nail a trick is to keep practicing it over and over again.

Get serious!

Most people skateboard for fun, and that's how it should be. If you have lots of ambition and determination, however, you could take your skateboarding to another level. Here are a few tips that might help you to take your skateboarding to the top.

Practice makes perfect

Don't think that when you have landed a trick once that is it. You will need to keep practicing if you want to become the next big name. Even established pros practice for several hours every day—they live and breathe skateboarding. But practice should be fun. If you start to feel sore, take a break and come back later.

Pushing an Ollie farther. Practice jumping objects, such as traffic cones.

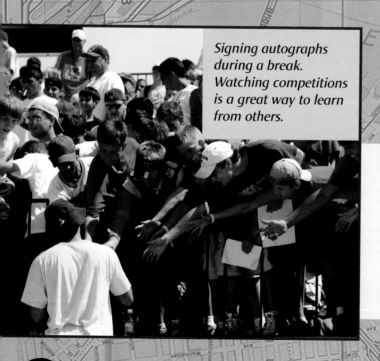

Signing autographs during a break. Watching competitions is a great way to learn from others.

Learn from others

Join a skate club, visit skateparks, and watch competitions as often as you can. That way, you will see others in action, pick up tips, and learn new tricks. Most top skaters have learned by skating this way and have then gone on to push themselves farther and develop their own style.

Get noticed, get sponsored

All top skaters are sponsored to help them meet the costs of traveling to events and to keep them tricked out with the latest gear. Many skaters are "spotted" by sponsors at competitions. This is by far the best way to be seen, and if sponsors think you've got what it takes, they may well offer you a deal. Another way to get noticed is to make your own skate video and send it to one of the big companies. Be warned, though: they are sent hundreds of videos, so you'll have to do something special to stand out from the crowd.

Danny Way gets himself noticed by pulling a spine-tingling Christ Air, invented by Christian Hosoi.

HOT HINT

Get to know the staff members at your local skateboard shop. They can be a great source of information about new gear and local clubs, competitions, and events.

From the left: Buckey Lasek, Sandro Diaz, and Bob Burnquest collect their awards.

Go for gold!

To increase your chances of skating stardom, you'll have to enter some competitions. Your local skate club or shop will probably have information about competitions happening in your area. Skateboard-scene Web sites and magazines also regularly feature competition announcements. If you work your way through the competitions, you could one day find yourself going for gold at the X-Games—how else do you think Tony Hawk and Danny Way became skateboarding legends?

FROM THE EDGE

"Being a pro skater would be a dream, but it is a lot of responsibility and commitment. I got into skating because it was fun. If skating was more of a job, perhaps I wouldn't enjoy it so much." Nick Jensen, street skater, Britain

Meet the pros

It is difficult to say who the best skateboarder is because all skateboarders have their own style. If you ask around, everyone has a personal favorite, but here are some of the big names you can't fail to miss.

Skating legend

The world's most famous (and most successful) skateboarder is Tony Hawk. He began skating in 1977 when he was just 9 years old and, by 14, had become a pro. By 16, he was the best skater in the world, and he dominated the sport for almost two decades. He has entered 103 pro competitions, winning 73 of them and coming in second in 19. Tony Hawk retired from competitive skating in 1999 but is still active in skating as a promoter and owner of top skateboard company Birdhouse.

Tony Hawk with a board designed by Birdhouse. He continues to influence the skateboard scene today.

To the limit

Rider profile:

Ryan Sheckler, or "Fly'n Ryan," was just 13 years old when he won gold in the X-Games Park event; he was the youngest X-Games winner ever. He went on to win nearly every major street event in 2003 and became the world's number-one street skater. Unfortunately, Ryan failed to pick up a medal at the 2004 X-Games.

To the limit

Rider profile:

Paul Rodriguez, or "P-Rod," turned pro at 17 in 2002, and in 2003, he rode off with bronze in his first X-Games Street event. He lost out that year to his hero Eric Koston, who, with four other X-Games medals, is one of skating's biggest names.

FROM THE EDGE

"Every kid that skates, that's their dream [to turn pro]. When your dream finally comes true, it's pretty tight. I remember when I was younger, for me and all my friends, our goal was to be pro. I'm not the kid looking up to the guys anymore. I feel like I'm in the cool club or something." Paul "P-Rod" Rodriguez discusses going pro

Catching up fast

Most pro skateboarders are men, but girls and women like to skate too and are catching up fast. Cara-Beth Burnside ("CB") was one of the first professional women skaters and has competed in men's competitions since 1991. She helped put women's skateboarding on the map. Other key women in skateboarding include Amy Caron, Lauren Perkins, and Elissa Steamer, who won the women's X-Games Street event in 2004.

FROM THE EDGE

"It's nice to have a handful of girls out there who are charging and learning new tricks. It's motivating for me; I like being around that. It hasn't been around for very long."
Cara-Beth Burnside (right)

Jargon buster

air — riding with all four wheels off the ground; short for aerial.

backside — when a trick or turn is executed with the skater's back facing the ramp or obstacle.

concussion — a severe blow to the head that often results in a loss of consciousness.

deck — the flat standing surface of a skateboard, usually made of laminated maple.

dropping-in — skateboarding down off the top of a ramp platform.

frontside — when a trick or turn is executed with the front of the skater's body facing the ramp or obstacle.

goofy foot — riding with the right foot forward, the opposite of "regular foot."

grind — scraping one or both trucks on a curb, railing, or other surface.

grip tape — a gritty layer stuck to the top of the deck to help a rider's shoes grip the board.

halfpipe — a "U"-shaped ramp of any size, usually with a flat section at the bottom.

jam — an informal event or gathering of skateboarders at a skatepark or similar location.

kickflip — a variation on the Ollie in which the skater kicks the board into a spin before landing back on it.

nail — to successfully complete a trick.

Ollie — a jump performed by tapping the tail of the board on the ground; the basis of most skating tricks.

rail — the edge of the skateboard; also, a handrail used for railslides.

railslide — a trick in which the skater slides the base of the deck along a rail.

regular foot — riding with the left foot forward; the opposite of "goofy foot."

street skating — skating on streets, curbs, benches, handrails, and other elements of street furniture.

trucks — the front and rear axle assemblies that connect the wheels to the deck and provide the turning capabilities for the board.

vert ramp — a halfpipe, usually at least eight feet (2.5 m) tall, with steep sides that are perfectly vertical near the top. There are now super ramps and mega ramps.

vert skating — skating on ramps and other vertical structures specifically designed for skating.

Find out more

Every effort has been made to ensure that these Web sites contain no inappropriate or offensive material. However, because of the nature of the Internet, it is impossible to guarantee that the contents of these sites will not be altered. We strongly advise that Internet access be supervised by a responsible adult.

www.longboards-skateboards.com
A site offering hand-carved and painted custom longboards. Also provides information on board care and the history of longboard development.

www.allgirlskatejam.com
Web site of the All Girl Skate Jam, established by Patty Segovia to promote female skateboarders. Features event coverage and an image gallery.

www.exploratorium.edu/skateboarding
Explores the science of skateboarding. Discusses tricks and equipment, and offers video footage of top skateboarders in action. Also contains a glossary of skating terms and tricks.

www.boarding.com/skate/index.html
Latest news, competition results, and useful tips. There is even a section that tells you how to build your own vert ramp.

www.spausa.org
The Skate Park Association of the United States of America (SPAUSA). Find out all about skateparks in the home of skateboarding.

www.skateboarding.com
The Web site of Transworld Skateboarding features online trick videos, live coverage of skateboarding events, and product reviews.

www.slalomskateboarder.com
For all you want to know about slalom skateboarding, including news, gear reviews, and the latest competition information.

www.bobstricktips.com
This is a great site to learn all those skateboarding tricks from the basic "Ollie" to the "360 Nose Shove It!" All tricks have photos and video clips to help you perfect them.

www.dannyway.com
The official Danny Way Web site. Find out about this record-breaking skater. Make sure you check out the mega ramp section with its amazing video clips.

www.nsc.org/library/fact/sktebord.htm
Skateboarding safety tips from the National Safety Council. Provides information on safety gear, as well as instructions on how to fall safely.

Index

50–50 Grind 24

All Girl Skate Jam 16
axle 7
  nuts 13

bailing 21
balancing 20, 21
bearings 6, 7
Birdhouse 28
Bullet Bird 6
Burnside, Cara-Beth ("CB") 29
bushing 7, 13

clubs 16, 17, 26, 27
competitions 17, 27
cruisers 9
curb wax 24
customizing 10, 13

deck 6, 7, 9, 10, 13, 30
  width 6, 8
DVDs 25

events, watching 17, 26

falling 21
fashion 5, 10

Gelfand, Alan 23
goofy foot 20, 30
grinds 8, 24, 30
grip tape 6, 13, 30

halfpipe 18, 30
Hawk, Tony 27, 28

history 4–5

jam 4, 16

kickflip 8, 25, 30
  "old-school" 25

Lindgren, Curt 25
longboards 9, 19

magazines 5, 27
maintenance 13
mountain boards 9
Mullen, Rodney 25

Nasworthy, Frank 5

Ollie 21, 23, 24, 25, 26, 30

Peralta, Stacy 23
public places, skating in 14, 15

rails 19, 24, 30
ramps 6, 8, 11, 16, 18, 21, 25, 30
regular foot 20, 30
renting 16
Rodriguez, Paul ("P-Rod") 29

safety 14–15
second-hand board 16
Sheckler, Ryan ("Fly'n Ryan") 17, 28
skateboard design 6–7, 8–9

skateboard gear 10–11, 16, 27
  clothing 11
  helmet 11, 15
  pads 11, 14
  patches 10
  shoes 10
  wrist guards 11, 21
skateboard shop 8, 11, 13, 17, 27
skatepark 4, 5, 8, 16, 18, 26
slalom skateboarding 19
sponsorship 5, 17, 27
stance 20
Stevenson, Larry 4
street boards 8
street skateboarding 6, 14, 19, 30
stretching exercises 12

tic tac 22
tricks 14, 18, 21, 22, 23, 24, 25
trucks 6, 7, 9, 13, 22, 24, 30
turns 7, 22

vert boards 8
vert skateboarding 6, 8, 18, 30

Wainwright, Danny 23
Way, Danny 17, 18, 19, 27
wheels 4, 5, 6, 7, 8, 9, 13, 22, 24
world records 18, 19

X-Games 5, 17, 19, 27, 28, 29